My Praise Journal

For Kids

ABOUT THIS JOURNAL

"Bring all who claim me as their God, for I have made them for my glory. It was I who created them" (Isaiah 43:7 NLT).

God loves us, all the time; when we have good days, and when we have yucky days. He loves us when we smile, cry, or laugh. He loves us when we do things right, and even when we make mistakes. He loves us when we are in a bad mood and when we are in our happy, crazy mood. He loves us all the time.

God also wants us to love Him back. He wants us to tell Him how we feel about Him and talk about all the good things He does for us. He wants us to think about Him. He wants to feel our love everyday, no matter where we are. In fact, that's what we were created for - to worship and praise Him!

Use this book to tell God what an awesome, cool, radical, sweet, and powerful God He is to you. He's going to love every page of it. Have fun with it, get creative, and then God with your own words!

Colleen Clabaugh
World Network of Prayer, Kids and Youth Prayer Coordinator

MY PRAISE journal

Date: _____

my day is going:
🙂 😐 🙁
—Say Cheese—

my scripture for today is:

_____
_____

I THANK G⊙D today for:

_____
_____

Why?

_____
_____
_____

My CREAtive word for G⊙d today is:

_____

It means:

_____
_____

Other th⊙Ughts about God:

_____
_____
_____
_____

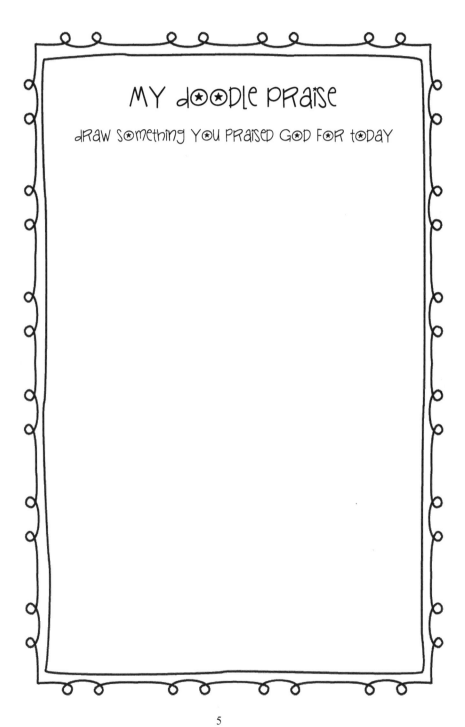

MY DOODLE PRAISE

DRAW SOMETHING YOU PRAISED GOD FOR TODAY

MY PRAISE JOURNAL

Date: _____

my day is going:
😊 😐 😞
─Say Cheese─

my scripture for today is:

_____
_____

GOD is so good when He...

_____
_____

Because...

_____
_____
_____

My happy word for GOd today is:

_____

It means:

_____
_____

Other thoughts about God:

_____
_____
_____
_____

MY S★NG PRAiSE

WriTE A SONG ABOUT GOd

MY PRAISE jOURNAL

Date: _____

my day is going:
☺ 😐 ☹
—Say Cheese—

my scripture for today is:

_____
_____

G⊛D makes me smile when He...

_____
_____

I smile because...

_____
_____

My CRAZY word for G⊛d today is:

_____

It means:

_____
_____

Other th⊛UghtS about God:

_____
_____
_____

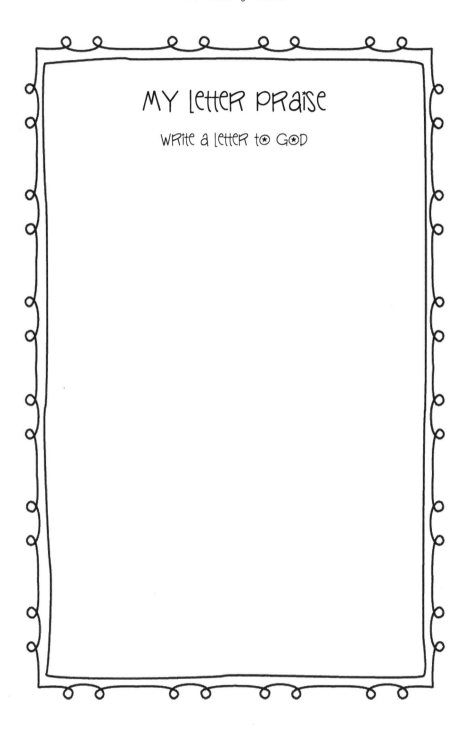

MY LETTER PRAISE

WRITE A LETTER TO GOD

MY PRAISE JOURNAL

Date: _____

my day is going:
😊 😐 😞
—Say Cheese—

my scripture for today is:

_____
_____

G☺D blesses me by...

_____
_____

this blesses because...

_____
_____
_____

My make-believe word for G☺d today is:

_____

It means:

_____
_____

Other th☺ughts about God:

_____
_____
_____
_____

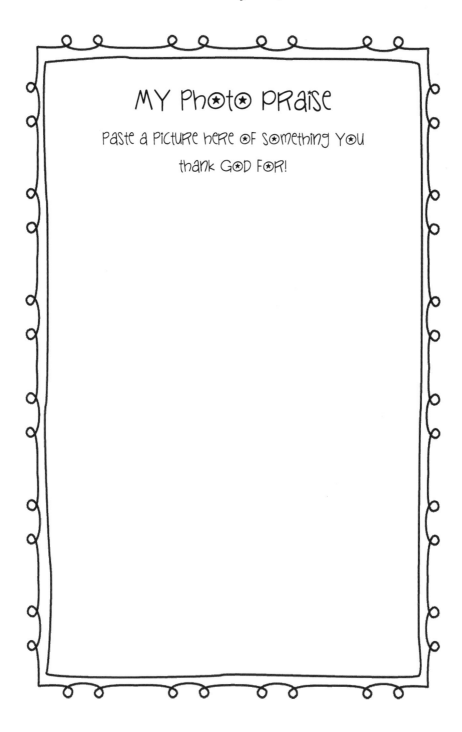

MY PHOTO PRAISE

Paste a picture here of something you
thank GOD FOR!

MY PRAISE JOURNAL

Date: _____

my day is going:
😊 😐 ☹️
—Say Cheese—

my scripture for today is:

_____

_____

GOD is so cool when He...

_____

_____

this amazes me because...

_____

_____

_____

My WORSHIP word for God today is:

_____

It means:

_____

_____

Other thoughts about God:

_____

_____

_____

_____

MY POEM PRAISE

WRITE A SHORT POEM TO GOD BELOW"

MY PRAISE JOURNAL

Date: _____

my day is going:
😊 😐 😞
─Say Cheese─

my scripture for today is:

_____
_____

I THANK G☉D today for:

_____
_____

Why?

_____
_____
_____

My CREATIVE word for G☉d today is:

_____

It means:

_____
_____

Other thoughts about God:

_____
_____
_____

MY dOODLE PRAISE

dRAW SOMETHING YOU PRAISED GOD FOR TODAY

MY PRAISE JOURNAL

Date: _____

my day is going:
☺ 😐 ☹
—Say Cheese—

my scripture for today is:

_____
_____

G⊛D is so good when He...

_____
_____

Because...

_____
_____

My happy word for G⊛d today is:

_____

It means:

_____
_____

Other thoughts about God:

_____
_____
_____
_____

MY S★NG PRAISE

WRITE A SONG ABOUT GOD

MY PRaise jOURNal

Date: _____

my day is going:

😊 🙂 🙁

—Say Cheese—

my scripture for today is:

_____

_____

GOD makes me smile when He...

_____

_____

I smile because...

_____

_____

My CRaZY word for GOd today is:

_____

It means:

_____

_____

Other thOUghtS about God:

_____

_____

_____

_____

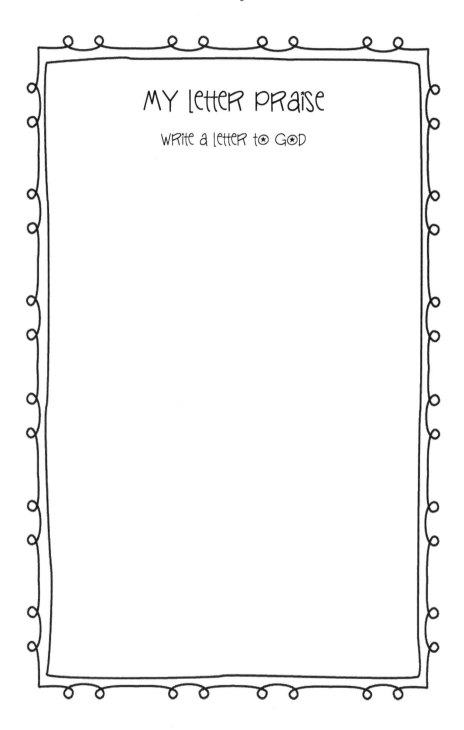

MY LETTER PRAISE

WRITE A LETTER TO GOD

MY PRAISE JOURNAL

Date: _____

my day is going:
😊 😐 😞
—Say Cheese—

my scripture for today is:

_____
_____

G⊙D blesses me by...

_____
_____

this blesses because...

_____
_____
_____

My make-believe word for G⊙d today is:

_____

It means:

_____
_____

Other th⊙ughts about God:

_____
_____
_____
_____

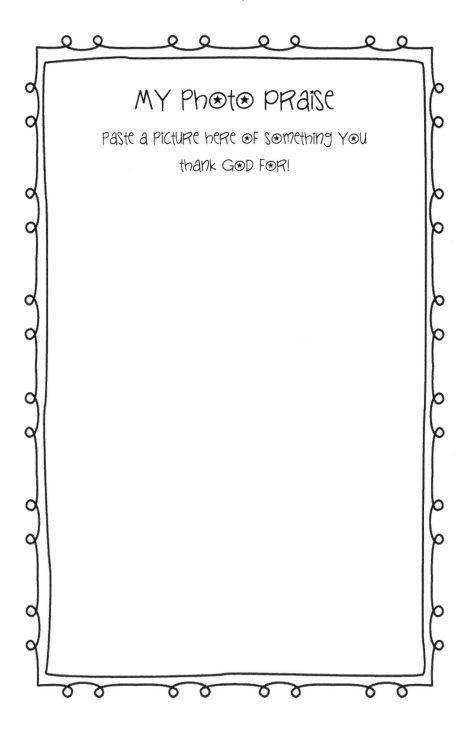

MY PHOTO PRAISE

PASTE A PICTURE HERE OF SOMETHING YOU
thank GOD FOR!

MY PRAISE JOURNAL

Date: _____

my day is going:
☺ 😐 ☹
—Say Cheese—

my scripture for today is:

_____

_____

G⊛D is so cool when He...

_____

_____

this amazes me because...

_____

_____

_____

My W⊛RShiP word for G⊛d today is:

_____

It means:

_____

_____

Other th⊛UghtS about God:

_____

_____

_____

_____

MY POEM PRAISE

WRITE A SHORT POEM TO GOD BELOW"

MY PRAISE JOURNAL

Date: _____

my day is going:
😊 😐 ☹️
—Say Cheese—

my scripture for today is:

_____
_____

I THANK G⊙D today for:

_____
_____

Why?

_____
_____
_____

My CREATIVE word for G⊙d today is:

_____

It means:

_____
_____

Other th⊙UghtS about God:

_____
_____
_____
_____

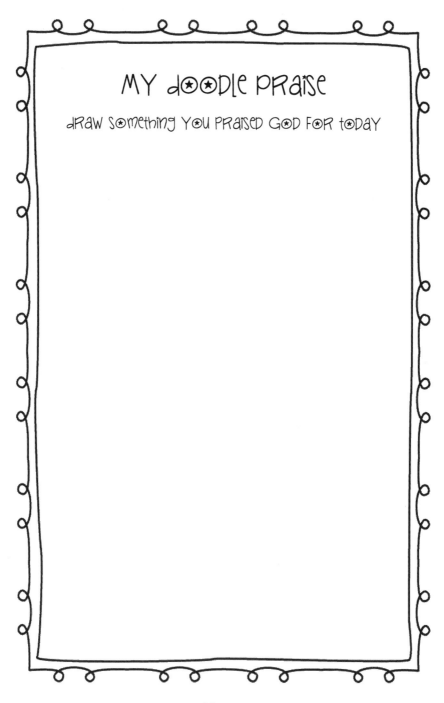

MY dOODLE PRAISE

draw something you praised God for today

MY PRAISE JOURNAL

Date: _____

my day is going:
😊 😐 🙁
─Say Cheese─

my scripture for today is:

_____
_____

GOD is so good when He...

_____
_____

Because...

_____
_____
_____

My happy word for GOd today is:

_____

It means:

_____
_____

Other thoughts about God:

_____
_____
_____
_____

MY S★NG PRAISE

WRITE A SONG ABOUT GOD

MY PRAISE JOURNAL

Date: _____

my day is going:
☺ 😐 ☹
—Say Cheese—

my scripture for today is:

_____

_____

GOD makes me smile when He...

_____

_____

I smile because...

_____

_____

My CRAZY word for GOd today is:

_____

It means:

_____

_____

Other thoughts about God:

_____

_____

_____

_____

MY LETTER PRAISE

WRITE A LETTER TO GOD

MY PRAISE JOURNAL

Date: _____

my day is going:
😊 😐 ☹️
—Say Cheese—

my scripture for today is:

_____
_____

G⊕D blesses me by...

_____
_____

this blesses because...

_____
_____
_____

My make-believe word for G⊕d today is:

_____

It means:

_____
_____

Other th⊕ughts about God:

_____
_____
_____
_____

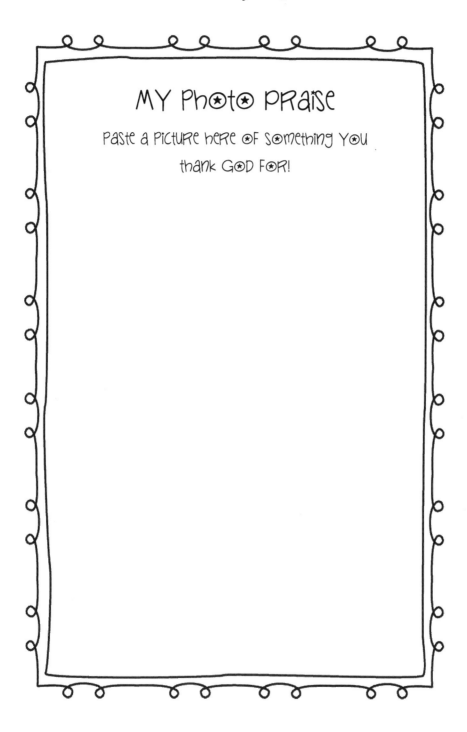

MY PHOTO PRAISE

PASTE A PICTURE HERE OF SOMETHING YOU
THANK GOD FOR!

MY PRAISE JOURNAL

Date: _____

my day is going:

😊 😐 ☹️

—Say Cheese—

my scripture for today is:

_____
_____

G⊙D is so cool when He...

_____
_____

this amazes me because...

_____
_____
_____

My WORSHIP word for G⊙d today is:

_____

It means:

_____
_____

Other thoughts about God:

_____
_____
_____
_____

MY POEM PRAISE

WRITE A SHORT POEM TO GOD BELOW"

MY PRAISE JOURNAL

Date: _____

my day is going:
☺ ☺ ☹
—Say Cheese—

my scripture for today is:

_____
_____

I THANK G☉D today for:

_____
_____

Why?

_____
_____
_____

My CREATIVE word for G☉d today is:

_____

It means:

_____
_____

Other th☉UGhtS about God:

_____
_____
_____
_____

MY DOODLE PRAISE

DRAW SOMETHING YOU PRAISED GOD FOR TODAY

MY PRAISE JOURNAL

Date: _____

my day is going:
😊 😐 ☹️
—Say Cheese—

my scripture for today is:

_____
_____

G⊙D is so good when He...

_____
_____

Because...

_____
_____

My happy word for G⊙d today is:

_____

It means:

_____
_____

Other thoughts about God:

_____
_____
_____
_____

MY S★NG PRAISE

WRITE A SONG ABOUT GOD

MY PRAISE JOURNAL

Date: _____

my day is going:

😊 😐 ☹️

—Say Cheese—

my scripture for today is:

_____
_____

GOD makes me smile when He...

_____
_____

I smile because...

_____
_____
_____

My CRAZY word for God today is:

_____

It means:

_____
_____

Other thoughts about God:

_____
_____
_____
_____

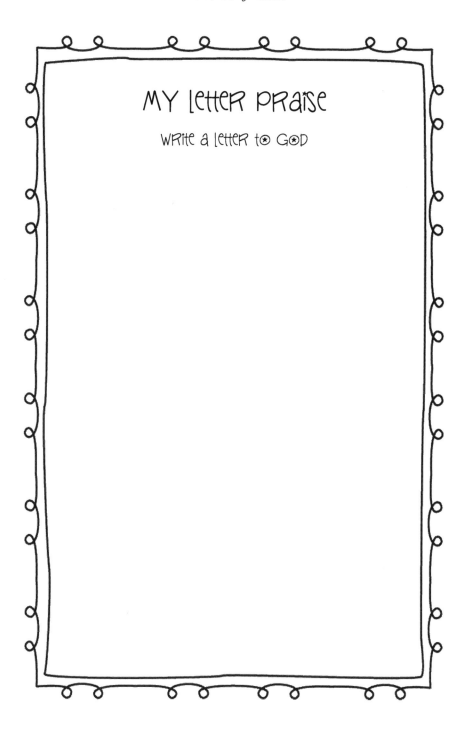

MY LETTER PRAISE

WRITE A LETTER TO GOD

MY PRAISE JOURNAL

Date: _____

my day is going:
😊 🙂 ☹️
— Say Cheese —

my scripture for today is:

_____
_____

G✪D blesses me by...

_____
_____

this blesses because...

_____
_____
_____

My make-believe word for G✪d today is:

_____

It means:

_____
_____

Other th✪ughts about God:

_____
_____
_____
_____

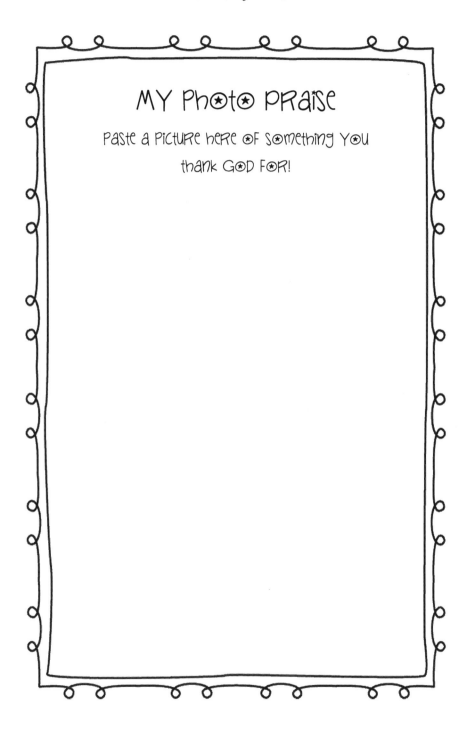

MY PHOTO PRAISE

PASTE A PICTURE HERE OF SOMETHING YOU
THANK GOD FOR!

MY PRAISE JOURNAL

Date: _____

my day is going:

☺ 😐 ☹

— Say Cheese —

my scripture for today is:

_____
_____

GOD is so cool when He...

_____
_____

this amazes me because...

_____
_____
_____

My WORSHIP word for God today is:

_____

It means:

_____
_____

Other thoughts about God:

_____
_____
_____
_____

MY POEM PRAISE

WRITE A SHORT POEM TO GOD BELOW"

MY PRAISE JOURNAL

Date: _____

my day is going:
☺ 😐 ☹
—Say Cheese—

my scripture for today is:

_____

_____

I THANK G⊛D today for:

_____

_____

Why?

_____

_____

_____

My CReative word for G⊛d today is:

_____

It means:

_____

_____

Other th⊛Ughts about God:

_____

_____

_____

_____

MY dOODLE PRAISE

draw something you praised god for today

MY PRaise jOURNal

Date: _____

my day is going:
😊 😐 ☹️
—Say Cheese—

my scripture for today is:

_____
_____

G⊙D is so good when He...

_____
_____

Because...

_____
_____

My haPPY word for G⊙d today is:

_____

It means:

_____
_____

Other th⊙UghtS about God:

_____
_____
_____
_____

MY S★NG PRaiSe

WRiTE A SONG ABOUT GOd

MY PRAISE JOURNAL

Date: _____

my day is going:
☺ 😐 ☹
— Say Cheese —

my scripture for today is:

_____
_____

GOD makes me smile when He...

_____
_____

I smile because...

_____
_____

My CRAZY word for GOd today is:

_____

It means:

_____
_____

Other thoughts about God:

_____
_____
_____

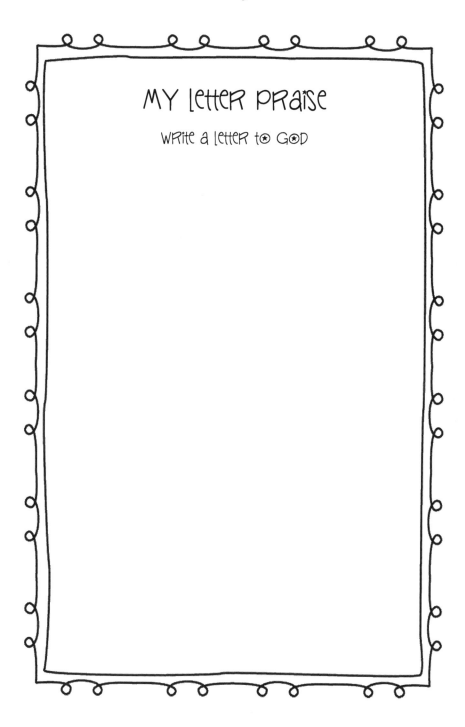

MY LETTER PRAISE

WRITE A LETTER TO GOD

MY PRAISE JOURNAL

Date: _____

my day is going:
😊 🙂 🙁
—Say Cheese—

my scripture for today is:

_____
_____

G⊙D blesses me by...

_____
_____

this blesses because...

_____
_____

My make-believe word for G⊙d today is:

_____

It means:

_____
_____

Other th⊙ughts about God:

_____
_____
_____
_____

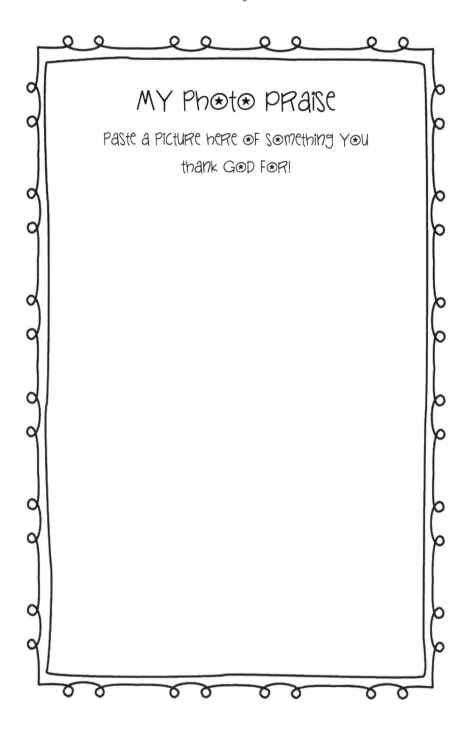

MY PHOTO PRAISE

PASTE A PICTURE HERE OF SOMETHING YOU
thank GOD FOR!

MY PRAISE JOURNAL

Date: _____

my day is going:
😊 😐 😟
—Say Cheese—

my scripture for today is:

_____

_____

GOD is so cool when He...

_____

_____

this amazes me because...

_____

_____

_____

My WORShiP word for GOd today is:

_____

It means:

_____

_____

Other thoughts about God:

_____

_____

_____

_____

MY POEM PRAISE

WRITE A SHORT POEM TO GOD BELOW"

MY PRAISE JOURNAL

Date: _____

my day is going:
☺ 😐 😖
—Say Cheese—

my scripture for today is:

_____
_____

I THANK G⊙D today for:

_____
_____

Why?

_____
_____
_____

My CREATIVE word for G⊙d today is:

_____

It means:

_____
_____

Other th⊙ughtS about God:

_____
_____
_____
_____

MY DOODLE PRAISE

DRAW SOMETHING YOU PRAISED GOD FOR TODAY

MY PRAISE JOURNAL

Date: _____

my day is going:
😊 😐 😞
—Say Cheese—

my scripture for today is:

_____

_____

G⊙D is so good when He...

_____

_____

Because...

_____

_____

My happy word for G⊙d today is:

_____

It means:

_____

_____

Other th⊙ughts about God:

_____

_____

_____

MY SONG PRAISE

WRITE A SONG ABOUT GOD

MY PRAISE JOURNAL

Date: _____

my day is going:

😊 🙂 ☹️

—Say Cheese—

my scripture for today is:

_____
_____

GOD makes me smile when He...

_____
_____

I smile because...

_____
_____
_____

My CRAZY word for GOd today is:

_____

It means:

_____
_____

Other thoughts about God:

_____
_____
_____
_____

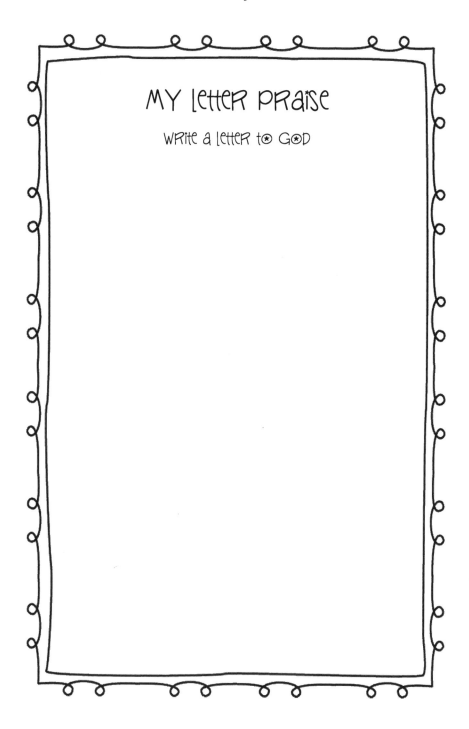

MY letteR PRaise

WRite a letteR to GOD

MY PRAISE JOURNAL

Date: _____

my day is going:
☺ ☺ ☹
—Say Cheese—

my scripture for today is:

_____
_____

GOD blesses me by...

_____
_____

this blesses because...

_____
_____
_____

My make-believe word for GOd today is:

_____

It means:

_____
_____

Other thoughts about God:

_____
_____
_____
_____

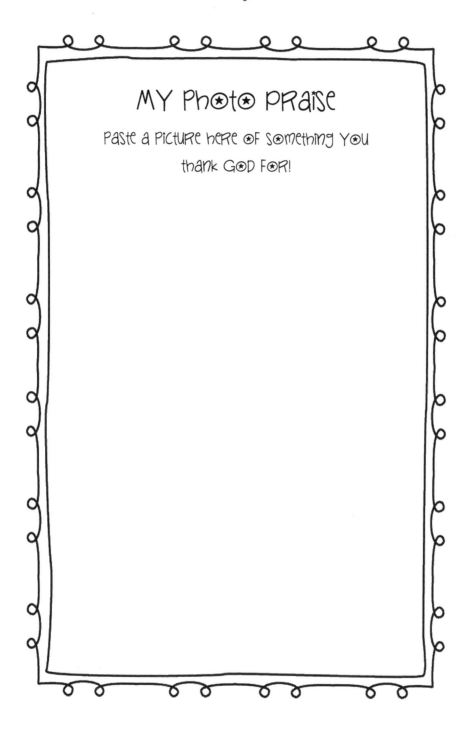

MY PHOTO PRAISE

PASTE A PICTURE HERE OF SOMETHING YOU
THANK GOD FOR!

MY PRAISE JOURNAL

Date: _____

my day is going:

☺ 🙂 ☹

—Say Cheese—

my scripture for today is:

_____
_____

GOD is so cool when He...

_____
_____

this amazes me because...

_____
_____

My WORSHIP word for GOd today is:

_____

It means:

_____
_____

Other thoughts about God:

_____
_____
_____

MY POEM PRAISE

WRITE A SHORT POEM TO GOD BELOW"

MY PRAISE JOURNAL

Date: _____

my day is going:

😊 😐 😣

—Say Cheese—

my scripture for today is:

_____

_____

I THANK G☉D today for:

_____

_____

Why?

_____

_____

_____

My CREATIVE word for G☉d today is:

_____

It means:

_____

_____

Other th☉UghtS about God:

_____

_____

_____

_____

MY dOOdLE PRAISE

draw something you praised god for today

MY PRAISE JOURNAL

Date: _____

my day is going:
☺ 😐 ☹
—Say Cheese—

my scripture for today is:

_____
_____

G⊙D is so good when He...

_____
_____

Because...

_____
_____
_____

My haPPY word for G⊙d today is:

_____

It means:

_____
_____

Other th⊙UghtS about God:

_____
_____
_____

MY SONG PRAISE

WRITE A SONG ABOUT GOD

MY PRAISE JOURNAL

Date: _____

my day is going:
☺ ☺ ☺
—Say Cheese—

my scripture for today is:

_____
_____

GOD makes me smile when He...

_____
_____

I smile because...

_____
_____

My CRAZY word for GOd today is:

_____

It means:

_____
_____

Other thoughts about God:

_____
_____
_____

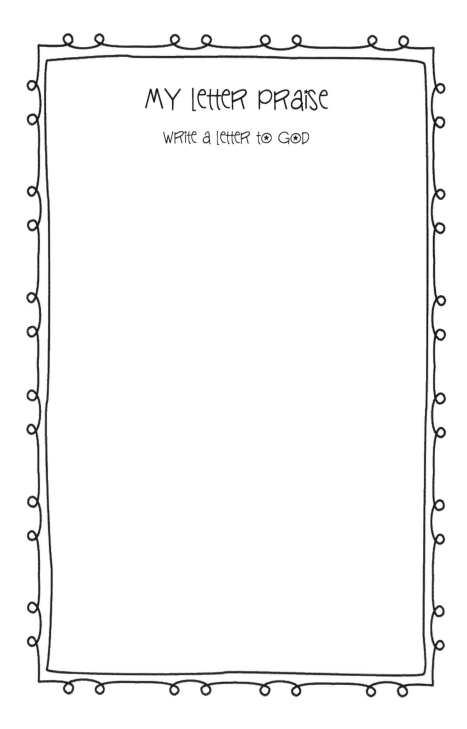

MY LETTER PRAISE

WRITE A LETTER TO GOD

MY PRAISE JOURNAL

Date: _____

my day is going:

☺ ☹ ☹

—Say Cheese—

my scripture for today is:

_____

_____

G☉D blesses me by...

_____

_____

this blesses because...

_____

_____

_____

My make-believe word for G☉d today is:

_____

It means:

_____

_____

Other th☉ughts about God:

_____

_____

_____

_____

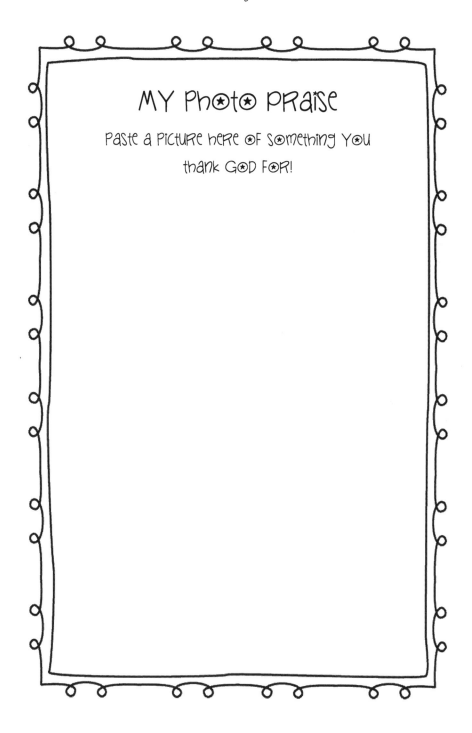

MY PHOTO PRAISE

PASTE A PICTURE HERE OF SOMETHING YOU

thank GOD FOR!

MY PRAISE JOURNAL

Date: _____

my day is going:

—Say Cheese—

my scripture for today is:

_____
_____

GOD is so cool when He...

_____
_____

this amazes me because...

_____
_____
_____

My WORSHIP word for God today is:

_____

It means:

_____
_____

Other thoughts about God:

_____
_____
_____
_____

MY POEM PRAISE

WRITE A SHORT POEM TO GOD BELOW"

MY PRAISE JOURNAL

Date: _____

my day is going:

😊 😐 ☹️

Say Cheese

my scripture for today is:

_____

_____

I THANK GOD today for:

_____

_____

Why?

_____

_____

My CREATIVE word for God today is:

_____

It means:

_____

_____

Other thoughts about God:

_____

_____

_____

MY dOODLE PRAISE

dRaw Something YOU PRAISED GOD FOR toDAY

MY PRAISE JOURNAL

Date: _____

my day is going:

😊 😐 😣

—Say Cheese—

my scripture for today is:

_____

_____

G⊛D is so good when He...

_____

_____

Because...

_____

_____

_____

My hAPPY word for G⊛d today is:

_____

It means:

_____

_____

Other th⊛Ughts about God:

_____

_____

_____

_____

MY S★NG PRAISE

WRITE A SONG ABOUT GOD

MY PRAISE JOURNAL

Date: _____

my day is going:
😊 😐 ☹️
—Say Cheese—

my scripture for today is:

_____

_____

G⊙D makes me smile when He...

_____

_____

I smile because...

_____

_____

_____

My CRAZY word for G⊙d today is:

_____

It means:

_____

_____

Other th⊙UghtS about God:

_____

_____

_____

_____

MY LETTER PRAISE

WRITE A LETTER TO GOD

MY PRAISE JOURNAL

Date: _____

my day is going:
😊 🙂 😞
—Say Cheese—

my scripture for today is:

_____
_____

G⊙D blesses me by...

_____
_____

this blesses because...

_____
_____

My make-believe word for G⊙d today is:

_____

It means:

_____
_____

Other th⊙ughts about God:

_____
_____
_____
_____

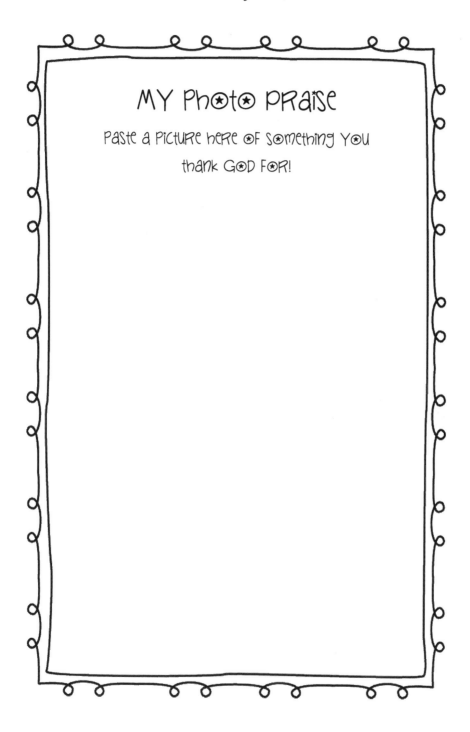

MY Ph⊛t⊛ PRaise

paste a picture heRe ⊛F s⊛mething Y⊛u
thank G⊛D F⊛R!

MY PRAISE JOURNAL

Date: _____

my day is going:

😊 😐 ☹️

—Say Cheese—

my scripture for today is:

_____

_____

G⊙D is so cool when He...

_____

_____

this amazes me because...

_____

_____

My W⊕RShip word for G⊕d today is:

_____

It means:

_____

_____

Other th⊕Ughts about God:

_____

_____

_____

_____

MY POEM PRAISE

WRITE A SHORT POEM TO GOD BELOW"

MY PRAISE JOURNAL

Date: _____

my day is going:
☺ 😐 😞
—Say Cheese—

my scripture for today is:

_____
_____

I THANK G☉D today for:

_____
_____

Why?

_____
_____

My CREATIVE word for G☉d today is:

_____

It means:

_____
_____

Other th☉Ughts about God:

_____
_____
_____
_____

MY DOODLE PRAISE
DRAW SOMETHING YOU PRAISED GOD FOR TODAY

MY PRAISE JOURNAL

Date: _____

my day is going:
😊 🙂 😞
—Say Cheese—

my scripture for today is:

_____

_____

G⊙D is so good when He...

_____

_____

Because...

_____

_____

My happy word for G⊙d today is:

_____

It means:

_____

_____

Other tho⊙ughts about God:

_____

_____

_____

_____

MY S★NG PRAISE

WRITE A SONG ABOUT GOD

MY PRAISE JOURNAL

Date: _____

my day is going:

☺ 😐 ☹

—Say Cheese—

my scripture for today is:

_____
_____

GOD makes me smile when He...

_____
_____

I smile because...

_____
_____

My CRAZY word for GOd today is:

_____

It means:

_____
_____

Other thoughts about God:

_____
_____
_____

MY LETTER PRAISE

WRITE A LETTER TO GOD

MY PRAISE JOURNAL

Date: _____

my day is going:
☺ 😐 ☹
—Say Cheese—

my scripture for today is:

_____

_____

GOD blesses me by...

_____

_____

this blesses because...

_____

_____

_____

My make-believe word for GOd today is:

_____

It means:

_____

_____

Other thoughts about God:

_____

_____

_____

_____

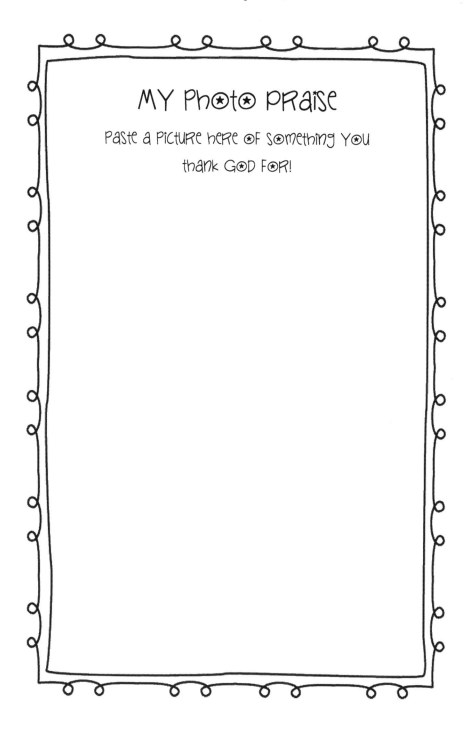

MY PHOTO PRAISE

PASTE A PICTURE HERE OF SOMETHING YOU
thank GOD FOR!

MY PRAISE JOURNAL

Date: _____

my day is going:
😊 🙂 🙁
—Say Cheese—

my scripture for today is:

_____
_____

GOD is so cool when He...

_____
_____

this amazes me because...

_____
_____
_____

My WORSHIP word for God today is:

_____

It means:

_____
_____

Other thoughts about God:

_____
_____
_____
_____

MY POEM PRAISE

WRITE A SHORT POEM TO GOD BELOW"

ABOUT THE AUTHOR

Colleen Clabaugh is the Kids and Youth Prayer Coordinator for the World Network of Prayer, an international prayer ministry.

She is a mother of two wonderful boys, a speaker, and a writer of many books and resources on prayer, and currently runs the Kids Prayer ministry at her local church.

Made in the USA
Middletown, DE
16 March 2022

62725439R00053